SYSTEMOLOGY
PROCESSING

POCKET EDITION

Published from
Mardukite Borsippa HQ, San Luis Valley, Colorado
Mardukite Academy & Systemology Society
for spiritual or educational purposes only

SYSTEMOLOGY PROCESSING

PRACTICES OF SPIRITUAL AWAKENING

A Basic Course developed
by Joshua Free
for the Systemology Society

THE JOSHUA FREE IMPRINT
JFI PUBLICATIONS

© 2023, JOSHUA FREE

ISBN : 978-1-961509-23-8

*Also available in hardcover as
"Fundamentals of Systemology"*

Pocket Paperback Edition — *October 2023*

mardukite.com

SYSTEMOLOGY is the
"New Thought" of the 21st Century.

It is the study of how
Spiritual Beings with unlimited power
became entrapped in the
Human Condition.

This study is an applied philosophy
— "A Pathway to Ascension" —
that charts our way back out,
freeing the True Self to experience
higher levels of existence again.

Systemology is the true science of the
"Matrix."

After more than a decade of
development, the "Fundamentals of
Systemology" are concisely explored
here in the first official
"Basic Course" on the subject ever
given by Joshua Free for the
Mardukite Academy.

It's time to discover
who you really are...
because you
were never "Human."

Fundamentals of Systemology
Basic Course Lesson Booklets

Lesson #1
BEING MORE THAN HUMAN
Rediscovering the Spiritual Self

Lesson #2
REALITIES IN AGREEMENT
Spiritual Life and The Universe

Lesson #3
WINDOWS TO EXPERIENCE
The Filters of Human Perception

Lesson #4
ANCIENT SYSTEMOLOGY
Wisdom From the Arcane Tablets

Lesson #5
A HISTORY OF SYSTEMOLOGY
Evolution of a Spiritual Science

Lesson #6
SYSTEMOLOGY PROCESSING
Practices of Spiritual Awakening

TABLET OF CONTENTS

INTRODUCTION
TO THE
"BASIC COURSE"

WELCOME, SEEKER!
YOUR JOURNEY ON THE PATHWAY
BEGINS HERE

This is a basic course in *Systemology*—specifically, the fundamental principles of *Mardukite Systemology*.

Quite simply: *Mardukite Systemology* is a new evolution in Human understanding about the "systems" governing *Spiritual Life*, *Reality*, the *Universe* and all *Existences*.

In many ways, *Systemology* is a 21st Century breakthrough that continues the legacy—and unifies the original pursuits—of early 20th Century *"American New Thought"* and other metaphysical schools of philosophy and mysticism. These are mostly all generalized (and often dismissed) in modern culture as *"New Age"* beliefs, though they are actually quite *"old"*—some even based on the most ancient known writings of discovered civilizations.

Mardukite Systemology was once concisely described as "an applied spiritual technology of the 21st Century A.D., based on spiritual wisdom from the 21st Century B.C." because of our use of *"Mesopotamian" Arcane Tablets* as source material for its foundations (and from which it retains a *"Mardukite"* designation).

The original *New Thought Movement* in America applied a "Western Civilization" approach to "Eastern" concepts—concepts that we now take for granted today, but of which were relatively unknown to the general population at that time. The movement sought to develop an "applied spiritual philosophy" whereby an individual could unlock their hidden potentials, untapped *"Knowingness"* and higher spiritual states of *Beingness*. These innate or native conditions of *Self* (as a *Spirit*) are blocked—or "fragmented"—by a "human" preoccupation with identifying *Self* as one and the same with the material body that it is merely using as a "vehicle" to experience (communicate and interact) within *this* Physical Universe.

Early *New Thought* work primarily emphasized practical "healing" applications (*mental healing, faith healing, &tc.*)—but at its very core, we may restate the ultimate pursuit or original focus was to "free humans *to be* their ideal native spiritual state."

This goal has been with us—lingering on the periphery of the "surface world"—for much longer than the existence of a *New Thought Movement*. In fact, for as long as "spiritual beings" have found themselves entrapped by a "Human Condition" and enforced to experience *this* "material existence" (fragmented from their true *Self*), a continuing pursuit has ensued to correct the situation—at least by those individuals still retaining enough *Awareness* to realize it.

Humans have been figuring on how to break free from the *"Matrix"* for a very long time. The desire or ambition to rise above the "standard-issue" Human Condition is already there. But the truth is that many other remotely similar "evolutions" of *New Thought* have dissolved into "multi-level marketing" schemes, "motivational pop-psychology" coaching, abusive "cult-like" movements—or heavily promoted books that skyrocket to the peaks of literary "bestseller lists" only to be discarded soon after and forgotten. They all share one thing in common: they all seem to capitalize on an innate desire or yearning we have to *"ascend"*—but, of course, without delivering stable results.

Even the most pious and well-meaning

philosophies and spiritual sciences have each fallen short of piercing the *"invisible barriers"* of perception separating *this* "Physical Universe" from any other "higher" existence—and with it, blocking our "way out" and the *Awareness* of our own true native state as an *Eternal Spirit.*

SYSTEMOLOGY:
21ST CENTURY NEW THOUGHT

Our *Systemology* is a new approach to *"Self-Actualization"*—completely relevant for the modern age and the future—and quite different from previous attempts or other traditions you might find.

Former attempts at overcoming *"barriers"* or *"gates"* of *reality* have included simply pretending that they don't exist, rejecting all material existence—all *time* and *space* —as an *"illusion"* and consequently losing the ability to actually *confront* the *reality* of anything *"As-It-Is."*

Our *Systemology* is also the answer to the "great mysteries" pervading the material sciences and natural philosophies; for they only seek to further qualify and validate the *reality agreements* made for *this* Physical Universe—and thus their level of understanding can never successfully pass the "barriers" either.

When applying our philosophy and techniques, the "systematic routes" outlined for an individual to increase their *"Actualized Awareness"* (and reach gradually higher toward their *"Spiritual Ascension"*) is referred to as *"The Pathway"*—and we call that individual a *"Seeker."*

At the start of *The Pathway,* early *routes* emphasize establishing a strong personal foundation of emotional well-being and mental strength before a *Seeker* is introduced to more advanced exercises and practices.

As a *Seeker* increases their *Awareness* in this lifetime, their spiritual "*Knowingness*" also increases—which is to say their sense of "*certainty*"; a certainty on *Life*, on this and other *Universes*, but more accurately, an increased certainty on *Self* as a practically unlimited "spiritual being" *having* an enforced restrictive "human experience."

One of the goals of "*Systematic Processing*" techniques in *Systemology* is to increase the ability of a *Seeker* to actually control and direct the "*attention*" of *Self* as a "spiritual being"—and as a result, *knowingly* increase command of the "human experience." This is a part of what we mean by "*Actualized Awareness*."

THREE STATES OF KNOWINGNESS

Raising a *Seeker's* level of *Actualized Awareness* requires, by definition, "bringing what is *hidden* (or not consciously known) up into the realm of *light* or *Knowingness.*" We might go as far to say, as an imperfect example, that there are three primary states of *Knowingness*: *actual knowing*, *almost knowing* and *not-knowing*.

Actual knowing is what an individual is conscious of and can easily recall as needed. It makes up our "surface" (or "above-the-surface") thoughts; what is *"actually known"* and available to *Self* for "inspection" or analytical thought. This includes what we have *certainty* on as part of our *reality*.

Then, there are other *things* "below-the-

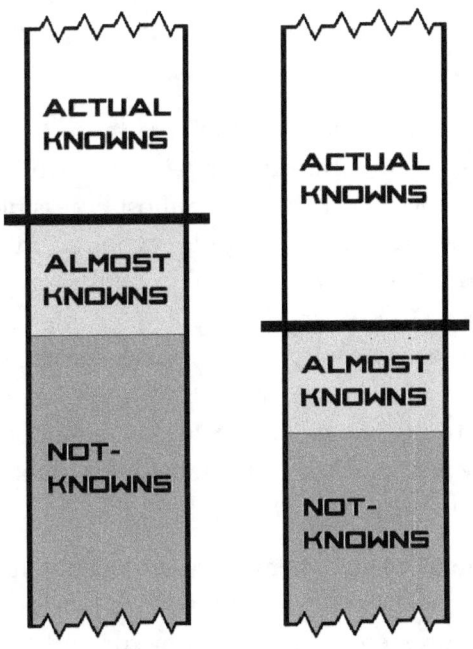

surface" that we do not easily remember (or have any *reality* on)—and these fit our other categories of *almost knowing* and *not-knowing*. The difference between these other two states is how *far* "below-the-surface" a *thing* is.

What you *"almost know"* are those *things* just "below-the-surface"—so *close* to the "surface" that they are almost accessible. This "gray area" includes what an individual is *uncertain* of. With a little assistance (*"Systematic Processing"* techniques), you can actually move a *thing* that is *"almost known"* to an "above-the-surface" state of *"actually knowing"* or remembering again. Only then may it be treated with any *certainty*.

There are also memories very deeply buried "below-the-surface." This includes suppressed data that is not currently accessible—and therefore, presently *"not-known."* Once again, there is a way to move *things* from this state into another state. For this to happen, the previous *"almost known"* *things* ("just-below-the-surface") need to be "purged" (at least partially) by *"resurfacing"* them into *"actually known"* *things*.

As more layers of *"almost knowns"* are *resurfaced* into *"actual knowns,"* more of what is *"not-known"* becomes accessible within the "gray area." *Systematic Processing* techniques of *Systemology* are intended to target this "gray area"—promoting increased *realizations* by elevating more knowledge to a state of *Actual Awareness*.

HOW TO STUDY
A SYSTEMOLOGY COURSE

Most *Seekers* study and practice *Systemology* at-a-distance and independent of the

"Mardukite Academy" or any "Master-level" mentors trained therein. This means that the *books* (and to a lesser degree, the *internet*) are the only means of direct contact a *Seeker* maintains with the "Systemology Society" during their studies.

It is quite common to have had negative past experiences with "education" and "learning"—whether in school or other type of instruction. This can sometimes inhibit an individual from pursuing a new *study* later on in their lifetime. However, simply following a few guidelines, ensures a *Seeker's* successful and positive experience when studying this course book—and, of course, the subject of *Systemology* as a whole.

To effectively study and understand a new subject (or a higher gradient of a subject), an individual must be "interested" in the material. A *Seeker* chooses to study *Systemology* because they "want" to, which is to say, on their own "*Self-Determinism.*" While modern society likes to enforce "agreement" (to further solidify a *reality*), a genuine "interest" and true "understanding" can only occur on one's own *Self-Determinism.*

Having established interest, the next *barrier* to understanding is "vocabulary" (words) and "semantics" (meaning). Any specific study, science or tradition is distinguished by the *words* used to communicate it. For true communication to occur, the intended "meaning" for each "word" used must be clearly defined and perfectly understood by the reader or receiver. We call this "*A-for-A*" or "*one-to-one*" communication.

Misunderstood words are the most common reason an individual abandons studying a subject. To relay a proper communication of *Systemology* concepts to a *Seeker*, we use very specific language in our course books. There are newer concepts that more obviously require defining when introduced; and some of our terminology uses familiar words, but with a different or specific meaning than when used elsewhere.

When a misunderstanding occurs, *Awareness* declines. These generally begin to "stack up" after the first occurrence and the level of interest and attention will also decline. This is how a "confusion" develops and the individual will get "bored" with the subject, feel tired, and unable to concentrate.

In extreme cases of confusion, there will be no future interest in studying or "looking at" something further. Feelings of "anger" and "sadness" may result (because one had originally *intended* on knowing something), followed by lower-level opposing "considerations" such as:

"didn't really want to know" or "it probably isn't very good anyways."

The misunderstood word that an individual passed in their study may not be immediately obvious. One solution is to return to the part of the material that was still interesting and enjoyable to read. When scanning around that area of text, there is likely to be a new word (or specific use of a familiar word) that is unclear, but was passed by unnoticed. All *Systemology* books include their own *glossary*. Using this *glossary* and a high-quality dictionary will help resolve this misunderstanding once it is located.

With "interest" and "understanding" secure, the next challenge of learning concerns making a subject *"tangible"*—which means handling it as a *"some-thing"* in the individual's personal *reality* or *Universe*.

Studying intellectual or "philosophical" subjects from a *book* requires excessive amounts of *"thought creation"* — of handling many conceptual images and ideas *"imagined"* solidly in one's "mind" in order to actually "look at" what one is studying. These also require a certain amount of present-time *attention* or *Awareness* to sustain a continual *creation*.

When an individual lacks "objective" examples (objects, graphic representations or direct experience) to examine, they may become "overwhelmed" by "mental-mass" if maintaining too many of their own *images*. This prompts feelings of being "worn out" or "weighed down" — and *considerations* that one "must take a break" or that the subject is "too difficult."

The obvious remedy is to supplement "book-learning" with objective or physical examples. Rather than simply studying or memorizing a series of "dry facts" from an "outside source" (and then returning to "ordinary" life), a student that does understand the material will take it up as their "own" *viewpoint*.

By taking the philosophies up as one's "own" *viewpoint*, the materially is effectively "owned" by the individual. They are not *looking* through a *lens* of someone else. The *"responsibility"* taken by this *ownership* means the freedom to apply information to everyday life and determine the truth of a matter for one's *Self*.

The final *barrier* to learning is the *knowledge* (or "know-*ledge*") itself—the *ledge* or *level* from which a person *knows* or *understands*. A "basic fact" could have many *levels* of potential understanding. To interpret *reality*, an individual "stands" on the *ledge-level* (or *gradient*) of *Knowingness* they have the most "certainty" on.

An effective education of any subject is

taught on a *gradient*. This is what is intended by introducing the study of something in "*grades.*" Rather than treating a subject as one total mass, true learning is achieved by increasing one's understanding on a *gradual* incline upward. The *ascent* to a mountaintop is not successfully achieved in one leap, but by targeting and reaching specific checkpoints along the way.

In 2019, the "*Grades*" were established for the "Mardukite Academy" to properly indicate what level of understanding a specific book or course is intended for. The entry-point to directly study materials of the Systemology Society at the Academy is "*Grade-III.*" Lower *grades* pertain to other *Mardukite* subjects treated separately from Systemology. Higher *grades* continue to explore the "theories and practices" of the Systemology Society as a complete "*Pathway to Ascension.*"

This *Basic Course* consists of a series of lessons (booklets) that teach the "*Fundamentals of Systemology.*" It is an appropriate entry-point for a new *Systemology* student. It is also applicable to more advanced *Seekers* wanting to increase their *certainty* of understanding at higher *grades* as well.

To study *Systemology* just like a student at the Academy: a *Seeker* reads through all instructional material in a *Basic Course* lesson (booklet) and then performs any practical exercises indicated at the end. Before continuing on to the next lesson (booklet), the material is read again and the light exercises are reapplied.

The second pass through the material is likely to result in different "*realizations*" (an increased *level of understanding*) than the first time. Exercises may seem more vivid or significant. *Seekers* should feel cheerful and confident in their *understan-*

ding of a section (or lesson) before pro-
ceeding even further on *The Pathway*.

YOUR FIRST STEPS ON THE PATHWAY

Systemology is a "holistic" approach to
understanding the human experience. It
is not actually a singular "subject" in itself, but rather, a way to "view" the many
"subjects" of *Life* and all *Existence*. Its
"scope" is not restricted to the rigidly
fixed *considerations* of any one "subject"
exclusively. Yet, for us to properly communicate its specific intended meaning,
Systemology does require its own unique
basic vocabulary.

The "basic vocabulary" and *"Fundamentals"* of *Systemology* are studied together
early on *The Pathway*. They are consistent
for the remaining upper-*grades*. It is our
understanding of them that evolves as we
progress.

The entire structure of *Systemology* rests on foundations of earlier material and earlier researches—such as those found in the earlier *grades* of Mardukite Academy. However, in 2019, new developments made it possible for a *Seeker* to start upon *The Pathway* without first spending years navigating around the pitfalls of other avenues and earlier *grade* subjects. As an extension of the original Academy, the Systemology Society continues to map and define the upper-*grade routes* of our philosophy.

The *Fundamentals of Systemology* are explored throughout the *Basic Course*. The critical foundations of its vocabulary and concepts (from *Grade-II*) were concisely collected in 2019 as an essay—"*Mardukite Zuism: A Brief Introduction.*" It is summarized below to provide a more complete introduction to the "lessons" of the *Basic Course*. Each "lesson" will go on to examine this data in greater detail.

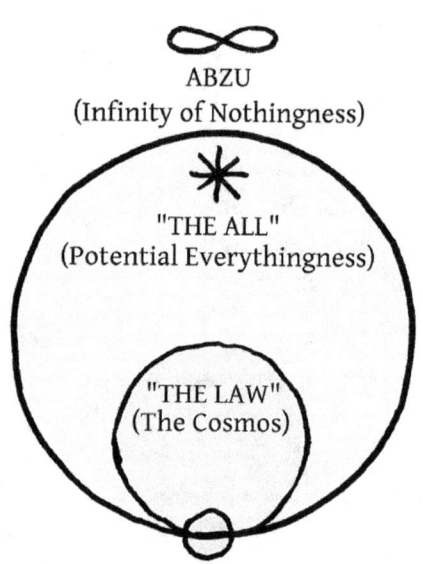

ABZU
(Infinity of Nothingness)

"THE ALL"
(Potential Everythingness)

"THE LAW"
(The Cosmos)

FOUNDATIONS OF SYSTEMOLOGY

Mardukite Zuism is a precursor to *Systemology*. It concerns an intensive archaeological study into the *Arcane Tablets* of Ancient Mesopotamia. Such tablet writings were once used to systematize an understanding of all cosmic knowledge— and they include the Babylonian *Epic of Creation*.

The *Epic of Creation* describes *ALL* ("ANKI") as separated into two *existences*: "AN" and "KI"—literally "heaven" and "earth"—which is to say *"spiritual"* ("AN") and *"physical"* ("KI"). Exterior to, and beyond, the *"potential everythingness"* of all *spiritual* existence and *physical* existence is only an Infinity of Nothingness ("ABZU").

In *Systemology*, we refer to the same two separate states of existence as *"Alpha"*

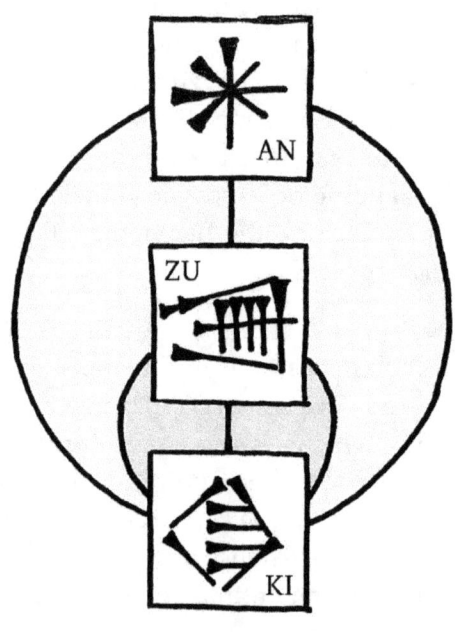

(*spiritual*) and "*Beta*" (*physical*). They are connected only by "*Spiritual Life Awareness*" or "ZU"—a term we have retained in *Systemology* (and for which *Mardukite Zuism* is named). Therefore, we have "*spiritual systems*" and "*physical systems*" connected by "ZU."

The "*Alpha*" *Universe*—of "metaphysical" or "spiritual" energy-matter—is not dependent on the "*Beta*" *Universe* to exist. The two exist independent of one another, except for a single channel or conduit maintaining a connection, which *is* the *Awareness* (the *Spiritual Life-Energy* or "ZU") of an "*Alpha-Spirit*."

"ZU" originates from an "*Alpha*" (*spiritual*) state, separate and distinct from the conditions of "*Beta*" existence that we experience as the *Physical Universe*. "ZU" is *Awareness*—the *Life-Force* or *Thought-Power* that "acts" or "impinges" on an "organism" in *Beta-Existence*.

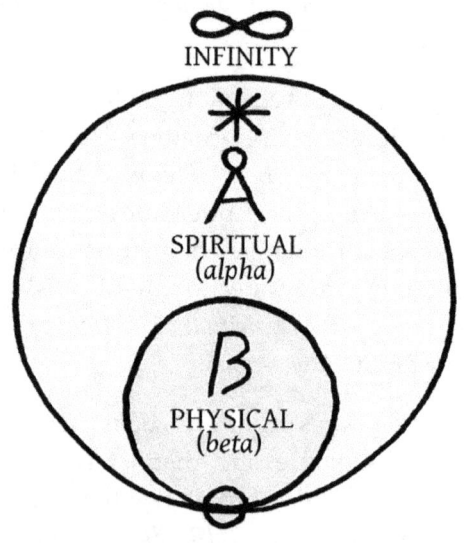

INFINITY

SPIRITUAL
(*alpha*)

PHYSICAL
(*beta*)

For example: the "intention" to read this book, or "commanding" a body to turn a page—those specific components are not actually a part of *this* existence. They are manifestations of a *Spiritual Awareness* (*Alpha*) acting upon an "organic body" (*Beta*). The *"Alpha-Spirit"* is the actual "Eternal" *Self*, which perceives and engages with *Beta-Existence* (*e.g.*, "Life on Earth") by using a "temporary" organic body or *"genetic vehicle."*

The *Alpha-Spirit* engages a *"ZU-Line"*—a *spiritual* "life-line" of *Attention* and *Awareness* ("ZU") energy—to an "organic body" or *genetic-vehicle* in order to directly experience a *"physical"* Beta-Existence.

We use the term *"Self-Honesty"* in *Systemology* to describe the original native "*Alpha*" state of true *Self-Directed "Beingness"* and crystal clear *"Knowingness."* Self-Honesty is the most basic "personality" or

37

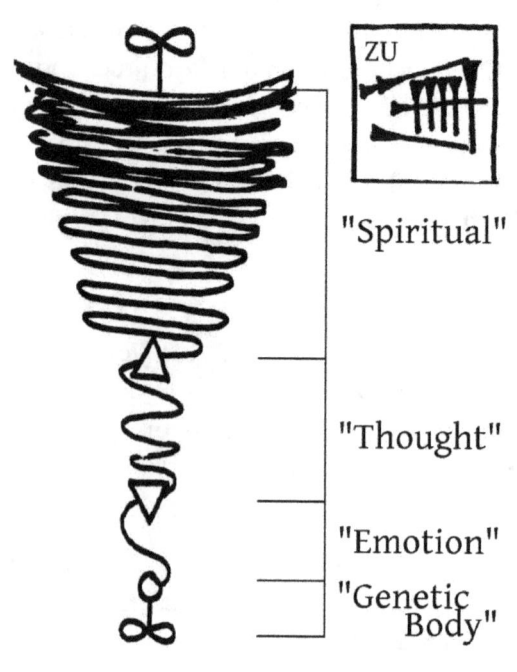

ZU

"Spiritual"

"Thought"

"Emotion"

"Genetic Body"

true expression of *Self* (*Alpha-Spirit*) as "I-AM"—a *Self-Determined* state that is *free* of artificial attachments, automatic reaction-response mechanisms, or enforced (*other-determined*) "reality-agreements" concerning the Human Condition.

Applying philosophic routes and systematic methods of *Systemology* in order to return *Awareness* of *Self* to its true "*Source*" is referred to as "*The Pathway*." Its structure is based on archaic "models" from the "Ancient Near East" (*Mesopotamia, &tc.*) and elsewhere—such as the "*Chakras*," the Babylonian "*Ladder of Lights*" (*Star-Gates*), and several versions of "*Kabbalah*."

For example: the Mesopotamians built "stepped-pyramids" as temples—called "*ziggurats*"—serving to remind us of the "ZU" bridging the *spiritual* and *physical* systems. Babylonians constructed *ziggurats* to correspond with *seven* primary "steps" or "*Gates*."

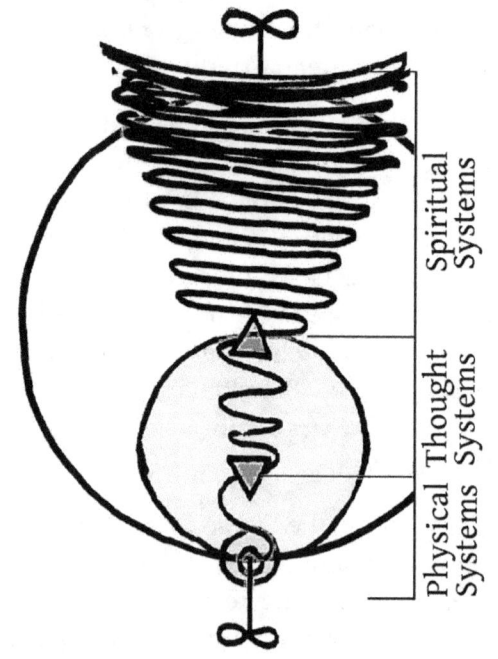

Spiritual
Systems

Physical Thought
Systems Systems

The "gradients" or "tiers" of the Babylonian *Ladder of Lights* represent *The Pathway*, because they define the *levels* of *Actualized Awareness* (and *Self-Honesty*)—the states of *Self-purification*—between the "standard-issue" *Human Condition* and *Infinity.* This is the *route* we travel for our *"spiritual defragmentation"* or *Ascension.*

BASIC VOCABULARY REVIEW PUZZLE

ACROSS

3. The standard-issue default manner of filtering perceptions of the Universe, as Self is experiencing it. (*2 words*)

4. The condition of being misaligned, broken apart, shattered, fractured, distorted, or otherwise separated into parts, compared to its original state.

7. A student or practitioner studying and applying Systemology philosophy.

8. The True Self or I-AM Awareness. (*2 words, hyphenated*)

10. The nature of the Physical Universe or material existence.

11. Another way to say "the agreement about what something is."

DOWN

1. The physical body, or any organic life, may serve as your ___. (*2 words*)

2. Regimen or routine of Systemology practices, techniques or exercises that increase Actualized Awareness of Self.

5. Returning to the original native state (or Source of the Spiritual Self) is known universally as ___.

6. A stream of energy connecting Spiritual Awareness to physical existence. (*2 words, hyphenated*)

9. The progressive journey taken in Systemology is referred to as "*The ___.*"

LESSON SIX:
SYSTEMOLOGY
PROCESSING

LESSON SIX
PRACTICES OF SPIRITUAL AWAKENING

The philosophy of *Systemology* may be applied to many fields and areas of everyday life. When *applied* within our tradition, practices and exercises toward "spiritual awakening" —or the *"Pathway to Ascension"* —are referred to as *"systematic processing."* Some of the inspiration behind this is derived from sources highlighted in *"Lesson 5."* But really this is the product of many years and innumerable sources.

"Systematic Processing" is only *one* part of our philosophy. It is itself an entire "methodology" for applying *Systemology* as a personal practice of techniques and exercises. We call it *"systematic processing"* because it is a precise practice (or "ritual") that *knowingly* mirrors or duplic-

47

ates the "systematic processes" of the *Mind.* It is too broad a topic to cover fully in a *Basic Course* lesson (booklet), but we can introduce its practice.

One of the basic goals of *"processing"* is to treat *knowingly* (at an analytical level of *awareness*) what is happening "automatically" or "compulsively"—or otherwise *unknowingly.* However, *processing* may be better understood as techniques aimed toward "spiritual development" and "ability enhancement." Of course, these *processes* or techniques are *applications* based on our *philosophy.* Hence: "applied philosophy."

Effectiveness of *systematic processing* is entirely based on our principle axiom that: The "I" or *Self* is an *Alpha-Spirit* operating from a *Spiritual ("Alpha") Existence* and employing a *Mind-System* to perceive the sensory experience of a *genetic-vehicle* (or *'body'*) that interacts in a *Physical ("Beta")*

Existence. This axiom *is* "The" *Fundamental of Systemology*—as already explored throughout the previous lessons (booklets).

Systematic Processing does resemble some practices from our predecessors in history; perhaps because it reaches for some of the same goals and ideals. It is, however, *not* synonymous with (or equivalent to) these other methods—meditation, prayer, mental healing, therapy, psychoanalysis, *&tc.*—at least not as they are commonly understood by the general (*exoteric*) public. Therefore, we tend to avoid using such terminology.

The most common application of *Systemology* is "*defragmentation*"—but this is only *one* use of "*processing*." *Defragmentation* is best understood with the model of "*knowns* versus *not-knowns*" given in the introduction. While many assume this means only a *knowledge* of "facts," the

49

same example could illustrate other uses of *processing*, such as a gradual increase of "dormant" (or forgotten) *"spiritual ability"* into *"actual ability"* &tc.

BASIC METHODS OF PROCESSING

An "applied philosophy" is really only as effective as an individual *understands* that philosophy and is able to *apply* it in practice. If a *Seeker* is unable to *understand* the philosophy enough to *apply* it, the logical solution is to find an individual that is professionally trained to *understand* it, until the *Seeker* has a *reality* on it themselves. For this, we developed the idea of a *"Pilot"* that could assist in guiding a *Seeker* on the *Pathway*.

This *"Pilot"* concept led to three basic "methods" of *systematic processing*, originally distinguished as *Piloted, Co-Piloted* and *Flying-Solo*. Over the course of many years of additional work, the meaning implied by these terms has evolved slightly during development. But, to briefly describe, they are:

Piloted Processing—an untrained *Seeker* is processed by a professionally trained *"Pilot."*

Co-Piloted Processing—two *Seekers* in training take turns processing one another; or a *Seeker* is processed by a trusted friend, reading from a book.

Flying-Solo—a *Seeker* in training processes themselves.

When first established in the 2010's, all *systematic processing* was intended to be *"Piloted"*—administered by a book-trained or Academy-trained *"Pilot"*—or *"Co-Piloted"* with a friend, or fellow *Seeker*, as *"Pilots-in-Training."* And this is exactly how *"Route-1"* (the first experimental method of *processing*) is presented in *"Tablets of Destiny Revelation"* (2019). More recently, *"Co-Piloted"* seems to apply to anything not done *"Solo."*

Soon after our debut publication, we realized the obvious limitations of a *Piloted* approach. We decided that when developing additional routes, they would need to apply to both traditional *"Piloting"* and solitary practitioners (who were *"Flying Solo"*). That being said, there *are* some *processes* (such as *"Route-1"*) that greatly benefit from having another individual present; yet others are just as productive when *"run" Solo.*

A *Seeker* working alone has only the option of being their own *Solo Pilot.* As such, they are responsible for all the "training" as a *Pilot*, and also managing the *"processing session"* for themselves as a *Seeker.* A certain level of *Self-Determinism* and *Actualized Awareness* must already be in place in order to successfully *"Fly Solo,"* since no one else is *present* to help maintain a *Seeker's* "presence" (*attention* and *Awareness*) *in session.*

The phrase "*Self-Processing*" is sometimes used in place of "*Solo*"—but this is not necessarily the most accurate term. Whether a *Seeker* is practicing alone or not, all *systematic processing* techniques in *Systemology* are "*Self-processed*"—which is to say, they must be *processed* by *Self.* And if it seems to you that *Systemology is* sometimes talking about software programming, or operating a computer, you're not alone; but it works.

A *Pilot* may assist in directing attention—or "redirecting" attention, if it strays—but the "command line" (verbal instruction) of a *process* is not a "magic spell" that "does something" by itself. To be effective, the *Seeker* must actually *apply* the "command line" of the technique as *Self* to *Self.* This is what we mean by "running

a process"—because essentially, a *Seeker*
is *processing* the "command" and resulting *data* as *Self*.

SYSTEMATIC PROCESSING SESSIONS

New *"realizations"* and increased *Actualized Awareness* improve a *Seeker's* handling of everyday life. This may be
enhanced through educational training,
but a more effective means of reaching
these higher ideal states is by combining
book-learning with actual practice of the
Systemology techniques and experiencing
the exercises we refer to as *"systematic
processing."* A few of these have already
appeared in the *Basic Course.*

To be strictly technical, the practice of
systematic processing is conducted in a
formal *"session."* We prefer the term "session" because of the common mystical

and/or religious connotations associated with the word *"ritual"* — or even *"meditation."* Our use of the phrase *"processing session"* is most accurate since it implies a specific duration of uninterrupted time set aside to focus on a particular procedure — or *process*.

Rather than conceiving the idea of a "session" as being similar to some "hourly counseling" in some other tradition, a "session" is a period of time for "running a process" toward an intended result or "end-point." A single "session" could last twenty minutes or two hours or more (taking breaks as needed, of course).

Proper procedures for conducting a "session" are followed whether a *Seeker* is *Solo* or *Co-Piloted*. This allows a *Seeker* to treat *systematic processing* as its own unique activity. For example: *"bathing"* is its own unique activity; but it also carries with it a whole regimen of "steps" that are followed in sequence—and which eventually become *"routine"* to the *process.* A *Seeker* practices to achieve that same level of familiarity.

That being said: even the fundamental practice of "starting a session," providing *"presence"* (*attention* and *Awareness*) to be "in session," then formally "ending the session," is a *systematic procedure* or *routine* in itself. To ensure effective processing, we add a step to getting *"in session."* A *Seeker* "scans through daily life" for upsets or problems that are "holding" parts of their *attention* or *Awareness*, even if only on the periphery.

When *things* are not handled analytically —or "above the surface"—they remain in suspension. A *thing* does not *disappear* by our withdrawing from it; it waits around, albeit out of view, to be seen *"As-It-Is."* Many aspects of living out the *Human Condition* have a tendency to keep our *at-*

tention suspended. Even when we go about performing other actions, the totality of our available *Awareness* is not generally present.

For example: we might be preparing a meal for our family, but at the same time we are thinking about problems at work, difficulties in managing the bills, and the driver that almost collided with us on the way home. It is also at these moments, when not living deliberately, that accidents can occur—because, the individual "isn't there" or their "mind isn't on it." Either way, they have withdrawn part of their "*presence.*"

Applying "*presence*" to a session is one of the most critical fundamentals of *processing*. Without it, a *Seeker* is not actually "*present*" to be *processed*. We aren't interested in *processing* a "body" or "computer-mind"; we are communicating directly with *Self*, the *Alpha-Spirit* that *utilizes* a *"Mind"* and *"Body"*—and *Self* maintains a "spiritual identity" that is in-dependent of a *"Mind"* and *"Body."* It is *Self* that we want *present* in session.

Systematic Processing operates by taking *knowing control* of an individual's avail-able *Actualized Awareness* and then in-creasing it—both the level of *control* and the available *Awareness.* This is similar to taking a small amount of *certainty* or *abil-ity* and "building up" from there. For a *processing session* to be effective, a *Seeker* cannot be withdrawing their *"presence"*—distracted by the upsets of daily life. This must be handled first.

It is no great mystery that having part of our *attention* on all of the aspects of living (that we hold at length on the peripheral boundary of our conscious *Awareness*) might inhibit our focused concentration or the achievement (or experience) of other "states." But, we can't simply igno-

58

re this fact, telling our *Seekers* and readers that we hope they feel better one day and come back to us when they do. We handle it *in-session*.

HANDLING IN-SESSION PRESENCE

Establishing *"in-session presence"* is not simply a preliminary step; it is a *systematic procedure* in itself. In fact, it is actually the *single* element underlying all other practices—of meditation, prayer, ritualism, *&tc.*—that produces any real *effects*. Of course, in other practices, these *effects* are misappropriated to some other *cause*.

The "location"—the environment or "setting"—is one of the first things to consider for establishing a session. This may be in an uninterrupted space outdoors, or in a quiet room. On occasion, the instruction or "command line" of a *process* may be directed toward a particular environmental focus—such as an "item" *in the room*, or a "person" engaged with others in a *public place*. These are indicators of the intended *setting*.

With the *setting* identified, the next step is making certain a *Seeker* is comfortable and relaxed within that environment. It is unproductive to attempt *processing* in an environment that is actively a source of "turbulence"—or worse, the very type of turbulence that is going to be *processed*. There is no reason for some cult-like disconnection; but a *Seeker* should have a "*retreat*" available to them while regaining balance.

Once a "safe location" is available, our next concern is the *Seeker's* comfort and familiarity with the material and intended practice. In traditional *Piloting*, this would include not only a confidence in the philosophy, but also the individual

("*Pilot*") administering it. When applied to a *Seeker* that is not also in-training, the total control of *processing* must be handled by a *Pilot* until the *Seeker* assumes responsibility for that control.

All of these factors boil down to what we consider the first elements of "*in-session presence*" that a *Seeker* provides to their exercises (*processing*)—the *attention* that they have available and are willing to provide to the session *in* present-time. And when we say "*presence*," we mean, quite literally, the *Awareness* of actually "*being present*" in the session. This "*presence*" *is* the unifying factor of all effective spiritual practices.

Other factors being considered, the actual "orientation" of a *Seeker's presence*—present-time *Awareness*—*with* the present space-time *setting* or environment, is the primary "opening procedure" for a *processing session*. An integral part of this procedure is determining if there are any aspects from daily life that are *inhibiting presence*. Sometimes the handling of these aspects alone is enough to qualify a complete session.

A *Seeker* handles the upsets or energetic-turbulence that is already present—or in stimulation—on the *ZU-Line* before attempting to *resurface* or reveal additional layers of *fragmentation*. Energy is always relayed as a "communication" (even internally for our "*perceptions*"); therefore, most upsets can be categorized as a type of "communication-breakdown" or "break in reality"—an unexpected interruption in the energy *flow*.

Different *processing* techniques target specific aspects of life. But, as a general rule —and in regards to *presence*—the basic idea is to *confront* ("come around to face") or *reach* rather than *avoid* or *withdraw*. Those *things* that we have 'blanked out'—

or choose not to look at—are still "energetic masses" surrounding our "field" of *Awareness*. All a *Seeker* really needs to do is "*acknowledge*" they exist so *attention* can shift off them.

To approach this *systematically*, a *Seeker* "spots" whatever incident or aspect is bothering them, then *looks* it over carefully and *analytically*. This may be done as thoroughly as is needed—noticing various things about it, but essentially *acknowledging* or *confronting* a thing "*As-It-Is*." This allows a *Seeker* to put some distance between themselves and the energetic-mass (*"problem"*) rather than treating it as though it were "present."

We return to our previous example of worrying about things while preparing a meal, even if *unknowingly*, which leads to an accident. What is taking place is that the individual is treating those other things as though they are *present* in the environment—giving them "attention-units" as though they are an imminent threat. Of course, by agreement, they are *real things, real incidents,* but *are* they actually *"present" in session?*

Once a troublesome aspect or incident is analyzed (as above), there should be some feeling of relief and an ability to refocus *attention* and *presence in-session*. A "problem" should *seem* "further" away rather than overwhelmingly close. If this is not the case, there may be another upset or distraction. If the troublesome aspect *seems* closer, then alternate *looking* at something in the incident and something in your environment.

This brings us to the other part of establishing *presence in-session*, which is "orientation with the present space-time" (or environment). Essentially, this is a part of what a *Seeker* is employing when *attention* is alternated by *looking* at something in the incident or situation and then something in the physical surroundings. We employ a similar technique as an "opening procedure" for all formal sessions as well.

In the case of handling "problems" or upsets, the alternation allows a *Seeker* to "unfix" *unknowing attention* on something that is being "fixedly" treated as "present" (*in-the-now*) when it is really *somewhere* else or a *past* situation no longer happening presently. These aspects that *attention* is *unknowingly* "fixed" to are what reduces available *Actualized Awareness* that is applied to any "present-time" activity—including *processing*.

Once *Awareness* is able to be focused or concentrated, this additional step—"orientation with present space-time" is essentially exactly what it sounds like: "orienting" *Self* in the present time and space of the session. This means bringing total available *Awareness* to the present-time location (space) of the session and the control of the "body" *in-session*. With regular practice these steps take less time further along the *Pathway*.

The experience of *"Presence In-Session"* will be familiar to continuing students and readers. Versions of sample techniques used as "opening procedures" of a *"Formal Session"* are given in the previous *Basic Course* lessons (booklets) as follows:

Lesson 1, Exercise 1 and 2;

Lesson 2, Exercise 1 and 7;

Lesson 3, Exercise 1, 2 and 7.

THE FORMAL SESSION

All *systematic processing* is practiced as part of a *"formal"* systematic processing session. Of course, there are some exercises

—such as those included at the end of each lesson (booklet)—that are effective even when practiced on their own. However, whether *Solo* or *Co-Piloted*, a *Seeker* applying our methods as a total *Pathway* toward *Spiritual Awakening* (or "*Ascension*"), benefits most by practicing techniques *systematically*.

A session is considered "*formal*" because it follows a specific pattern or ceremonial formula of *formal* action and communication. There is a *formal* "beginning" and "ending" of a *systematic session*. Several *processes* may occur within a single session; each one "started" and "stopped" (in turn) as a *formal* act.

Traditional *Piloted Processing* differs from *Flying-Solo*, but the basic formula for a "*Formal Session*" is the same. In *Piloted* (or *Co-Piloted*) *processing*, the factor of *communication* between a *Pilot* and *Seeker* must be handled in addition to the *session* and *processes*. In *Solo-Processing*, the *communication* of a *process in-session* is all handled "internally"—between *Self* and the *"Mind"* (and *"Body"*) without being directed by a *"Co-Pilot."*

A precise instruction for a *process* is referred to as a *"processing command line"* (or "PCL"). This is named for the act of "inputting" a "command line" into a "computing device." In traditional *Piloted* sessions, a *Seeker* receives a communicated "command line" from the *Pilot*, then communicates the "command" to the *Mind* as *Self*. *Solo* or not, a *Seeker* directs their own *Mind* to *process* the "command"; another *Pilot* only assists this.

A *"processing command line"* (PCL), by itself, is *not* a "magical incantation" that spontaneously produces *actualization*. A misunderstood one, however, *does* have the "power" to slow or stop forward progress. A *Seeker* that is studying/training on their own usually does not have an issue *in-session*, because they can get a clear understanding beforehand. A *Pilot* is responsible for making sure of this for a *Seeker* not in-training.

For example: if you take someone randomly off the street and ask, *"would it be okay if we start this session?"* Well, there is obviously little context there. Even an individual that is interested in getting *processed* might not understand the use of the word "session" at first unless some of the basic *Systemology* philosophy is explained. A *Solo-Pilot* simply accepts total responsibility for attaining this understanding for themselves.

Solo-Sessions may be run *"silently"* as direct "mental commands"—but this is not an absolute rule. In either case, a *Seeker* should be focused on handling the commands directly and not *imagine* also *being* "another person" that is giving themselves the commands. Such "add-ons" are unnecessary and counter-productive. However, the same formal session "script" that a *Co-Pilot* communicates, a *Solo-Pilot* reads and *Self-Directs*.

The whole purpose of a *processing session* surrounds the idea of an individual focusing and increasing their *Self-directed* control—or *Self-determinism*. In order to retain this focus, every *one* PCL of a formal session or *process* must have a *Seeker's* total *presence*. This level of focused direction is one benefit of traditional *Piloting*—but in *Solo*, a *Seeker* is instructed to keep a piece of paper over portions of a script/process not yet used.

What follows is a basic script from a *Formal Session* used for training purposes at the Academy. It is a guideline only—based on a transcript of a traditional *Piloted Processing Session*. It is, however, easily adapted to use for *Flying-Solo* once a *Seeker* has practiced the exercises used for achieving *presence in-session*.

1. BEGINNING THE SESSION

"Would it be okay with you if we begin this session now?"

"Okay."

"Start of session."

2. OPENING PROCEDURES

A. Presence In-Session

"Is there anything going on that might keep your attention from being present in-session?"

(if *"no,"* acknowledge and go to B.; if *"yes,"* continue below)

"Okay. Tell me about it."

"Alright. How does that problem seem to you now?"

(if *"further away"* or handled, acknowledge and go to B.; if *"closer"* or more turbulent, continue below)

"Spot something in the incident; Spot something in the room."

(this alternating command line is repeated as needed)

B. Orientation in Present Space-Time

"Get the sense of you making that body sit in that chair."

"Okay. Get a sense of the floor beneath your feet."

"Do you have that real good?"

(if *"no,"* acknowledge and repeat *A.*; if *"yes,"* continue below)

"Recall a time something seemed real to you."

"Tell me something you notice about it."

"Look around and spot something in the room."

"What do you notice about that?"

(these last four command lines are repeated in series as needed; acknowledge and continue below)

C. Control of Body and Mind In-Session

(two dissimilar objects—here given as *"Item-1"* and *"Item-2"*—are presented and placed within reach; or alternatively, at two distant points in the room, in which a command line for "walking" between them would be inserted)

"Pick up Item-1."

"Tell me about its weight."

"Tell me about its color."

"Tell me about its texture."

"Put it down."

"Pick up Item-2."

"Tell me about its weight."

"Tell me about its color."

"Tell me about its texture."

"Put it down."

(this series of command-lines may be repeated several times; when there is no communication-lag for several full series, and duplicate answers are reoccurring, acknowledge and continue below)

"Choose an object. Decide when you are going to reach for it. Then make that body pick it up."

"Now decide when you are going to put it down. Then make that body put it back where it was."

(repeat as needed; when there is no communication-lag for a full series of command lines, acknowledge and continue below)

"Close your eyes. Put all of your attention on the upper two back corners of the room and just get real interested in them for a while."

(if there are no visible signs of "strain" after two minutes, acknowledge and continue below)

D. Establishing the Session

"Do you have any goals for this session, or anything in particular you want to address?"

(acknowledge, then start a process)

3. <u>STARTING A PROCESS</u>

"I would like to start a process; would that be okay?"

"Alright. The command lines are ---. Does this make sense?"

(if *"no,"* clear up any misunderstood words; if *"yes,"* start the process)

4. <u>CHANGING A PROCESS</u>

(only the wording in a command line may be changed to make it more workable for a *Seeker*; to change processes altogether, the present process must reach an end-point)

Example: a Seeker expresses inability to "imagine" or visualize imagery.

"Okay. Well, just 'get a sense' of..." or *"Just 'get the idea' of..."*

Example: a Seeker expresses discomfort (or withdrawal from) recalling a particular incident.

"That's fine. What part of that incident 'could' you confront?"

5. <u>STOPPING A PROCESS</u>

(when an end-point has been reached on a repetitive-style process)

"We'll just run this process a couple more times if that's okay with you?"

(general process is run two more times)

"Okay. Is there anything you would like to tell me before we end this process?"

(**or**, if an end-point "realization" is communicated from a process)

"Alright. Very good."

(the formal end of a particular process requires a command-line)

"End of process."

6. <u>ENDING THE SESSION</u>

(once a process, or series of processes, is completed)

"Is there anything you would like to tell me before we end this session?"

(if *"yes,"* acknowledge and handle it with communication before ending the session; if *"no,"* continue below)

"Would it be okay if we ended this session now?"

"Okay."

"End of session."

YOUR FUTURE AND SYSTEMOLOGY

The *Systemology Society* has established several "levels" of *processing* that are available for study and practice. There are literally *hundreds* of techniques and *systematic processes* that a *Seeker* may apply to their own journey on the *Pathway to Spiritual Ascension*. This *Basic Course* allows that additional study to be more effective; because all the *processes* in the world do not replace a *Seeker's* ability to provide *presence in-session*.

Seekers that have completed the *Basic Course* series may be wondering what to study and practice next. The new *"Professional Course"* series provides training and processing for the entire *Pathway* leading up to the upper-most levels of our *Systemology* work. It consists of approximately *30* progressive lessons (booklets)—similar in style to the presentation of the *six* in this *Basic Course* series on *"Fundamentals of Systemology."*

PRACTICE EXERCISES

1. Practice speaking the command lines of a *Formal Session*. This will familiarize yourself with the flow of a *Formal Session*, even for *Solo-Processing*. Do not actually "perform" the steps at this point; simply read the lines and speak them out loud. Start with only Step-1 *and* Step-6 ("Beginning" and "Ending" a *Formal Session*). Then add each part of Step-2 ("Opening Procedures") one at a time. [The parts of Step-2 are distinguished by letters A, B, C and D.] Finally, you may include the examples for the remaining steps regarding handling of a particular process, thereby rehearsing the entire script.

2. Practice speaking the command lines for Step-1 *and* Step-6 ("Beginning" and "Ending" a *Formal Session*); but this time with actual intention. Get the idea or sense of actually putting yourself into, and coming out of, a *Formal Session*. Do not "perform" any additional steps at this point. Simply get the idea of setting aside a particular period of time in space to conduct a *Formal Session*.

3. Refer to the previous exercise; but this time *silently* use intention to "Begin" and "End" a *Session*.

4. In this exercise: "Begin" (Step-1) a Formal Session for yourself; then practice performing each part (letter) of the "Opening Procedure" (Step-2) as a Solo exercise in its own session until you are satisfied. Be sure to include the "End" (Step-6) for each practice

session. Refer to the material in this *Basic Course* lesson (booklet) for assistance on achieving "*Presence In-Session.*"

5. Practice communicating a *Formal Session* with actual intention, to a friend or family member. Use Step-1; Step-2, A, B, C; Step-5 (for when an *end-realization* has occurred); and Step-6. No other steps or processes need to be run for this exercise. This practice should be considered a *real* exercise; and you can encourage the other person to actually perform the procedure. Even without the inclusion of additional processing, this basic "regimen" or "routine" has the potential to provide beneficial results—and this includes individuals not studying, or otherwise practicing, *Systemology.*

Certificate of Completion

This certificate is awarded to

_____

for the successful completion of
the Mardukite Academy Basic Course on

The Fundamentals of Systemology

GLOSSARY

actualization : to make actual, not just potential; to bring into full solid Reality; to realize fully in *Awareness* as a "thing."

agreement (reality) : unanimity of opinion of what is "thought" to be known; an accepted arrangement of how things are; things we consider as "real" or as an "is" of "reality"; a consensus of what is real as made by standard-issue (common) participants; what an individual contributes to or accepts as "real"; in *Systemology*, a synonym for "*reality.*"

alpha : the first, primary, basic, superior or beginning of some form; in *Systemology*, referring to the state of existence operating on spiritual archetypes and postulates, will and intention "exterior" to the low-level condensation and solidarity of energy and matter as the 'physical universe'.

alpha-spirit : a "spiritual" *Life*-form; the "true" *Self* or I-AM; the *individual*; the spiritual (*alpha*) *Self* that is animating the (*beta*) physical body or "*genetic vehicle*" using a continuous *Lifeline* of spiritual ("*ZU*") energy; an individual spiritual (*alpha*) entity possessing no physical mass or measurable waveform (motion) in the Physical Universe as itself, so it animates the (*beta*) physical body or "*genetic vehicle*" as a catalyst to experience *Self*-determined causality in effect within the *Physical Universe*; a singular unit or point of *Spiritual Awareness* that is *Aware* that it is *Aware*.

alpha thought : the highest spiritual *Self-determination* over creation and existence exercised by an Alpha-Spirit; the Alpha range of pure *Creative Ability* based on direct postulates and considerations of *Beingness*; spiritual qualities comparable to "thought" but originating in Alpha-existence (at "6.0") independently superior to a *beta-anchored* Mind-System, although an Alpha-Spirit may use Will ("5.0") to carry the intentions of a postulate or consideration ("6.0") to the Master Control Center ("4.0").

ascension : actualized *Awareness* elevated to the point of true "spiritual existence" exterior to *beta existence*. An "Ascended Master" is one who has returned to an incarnation on Earth as an inherently *Enlightened One*, demonstrable in their actions—they have the ability to *Self-direct* the "Spirit" as *Self* and maintain consciousness beyond this existence as a personal identity continuum with the same *Self-directed* control and communication of Will-Intention that is exercised, actualized and developed deliberately during one's present incarnation.

associative knowledge : significance or meaning of a facet or aspect assigned to (or considered to have) a direct relationship with another facet; to connect or relate ideas or facets of existence with one another; a reactive-response image, emotion or conception that is suggested by (or directly accompanies) something other than itself; in traditional systems logic, an equivalency of significance or meaning between facets or sets that are grouped together, such as in *(a + b) + c = a + (b + c)*; in NexGen Systemology, erroneous associative knowledge is assignment of the same value to all facets or parts considered as related (even when they are not actually so), such as in *a = a, b = a, c = a* and so forth without distinction.

attention : active use of *Awareness* toward a specific aspect or thing; the act of "attending" with the presence of *Self*; a direction of focus or concentration of *Awareness* along a particular channel or conduit or toward a particular terminal node or communication termination point; the Self-directed concentration of personal energy as a combination of observation, thought-waves and consideration; focused application of *Self-Directed Awareness*.

awareness : the highest sense of-and-as Self in knowing and being as I-AM (the *Alpha-Spirit*); the extent of beingness directed as a POV experienced by Self as knowingness.

beta (awareness) : all consciousness activity ("*Awareness*") in the "Physical Universe" (KI) or else *beta-existence*; *Awareness* within the range of the *genetic-body*, including material thoughts, emotional responses and physical motors; personal *Awareness* of physical energy and physical matter moving through physical space and experienced as "time"; the *Awareness* held by *Self* that is restricted to a physical organic *Lifeform* or "*genetic vehicle*" in which it experiences causality in the *Physical Universe*.

beta (existence) : all manifestation in the "Physical Universe" (KI); the "Physical" state of existence consisting of vibrations of physical energy and physical matter moving through physical space and experienced as "time"; the conditions of *Awareness* for the *Alpha-spirit* (*Self*) as a physical organic *Lifeform* or "*genetic vehicle*" in which it experiences causality in the *Physical Universe*.

beta-defragmentation : toward a state of *Self-Honesty* in regards to handling experience of the "Physical Universe" (*beta-existence*); an applied spiritual philosophy (or technology) of Self-Actualization

channel : a specific stream, course, current, direction or route; to form or cut a groove or ridge or otherwise guide along a specific course; a direct path; an artificial aqueduct created to connect two water bodies or water or make travel possible.

circuit : a circular path or loop; a closed-path within a system that allows a flow; a pattern or action or wave movement that follows a specific route or potential path only.

condense (condensation) : the transition of vapor to liquid; denoting a change in state to a more substantial or solid condition; leading to a more compact or solid form.

consideration : careful analytical reflection of all aspects; deliberation; determining the significance of a "thing" in relation to similarity or dissimilarity to other "things"; evaluation of facts and importance of certain facts; thorough examination of all aspects related to, or important for, making a decision; the analysis of consequences and estimation of significance when making decisions.

continuity : being a continuous whole; a complete whole or "total round of"; the balance of the equation ["−120" + "120" = "0" &tc.]; an apparent unbroken interconnected coherent whole; also, as applied to Universes in *Systemology*, the lowest base consideration of space-time or commonly shared level of energy-matter apparent in an existence, or else the lowest degree of solidity or condensation whereby all mass that exists is identifiable or communicable with all other mass that exists; represented as "0" on the *Standard Model* for the Physical Universe (*beta-existence*), a level of existence that is below Human emotion, comparable to the solidity of "rocks" and "walls" and "inert bodies."

defragmentation : the *reparation* of wholeness; collecting all dispersed parts to reform an original whole; a process of removing "*fragmentation*" in data or knowledge to provide a clear understanding; applying techniques and processes that promote a *holistic* interconnected *alpha* state, favoring observational *Awareness* of continuity in all spiritual and physical systems; in *Systemology*, a "*Seeker*" achieving an actualized state of basic "*Self-Honest Awareness*" is said to have completed *beta-defragmentation*, whereas *Alpha-defragmentation* is the rehabilitation of the *creative ability*, managing the *Spiri-*

tual Timeline and the POV of *Self* as Alpha-Spirit (I-AM).

existence : the *state* or fact of *apparent manifestation*; the resulting combination of the Principles of Manifestation: consciousness, motion
and substance; continued *survival*; that which
independently exists.

exterior : outside of; on the outside; in *Systemology*, we mean specifically the POV of *Self* that
is *'outside of'* the *Human Condition,* free of the
physical and mental trappings of the Physical
Universe; a metahuman range of consideration;
see also *'Zu-Vision'*.

external : a force coming from outside; information received from outside sources; in *Systemology*, the objective *'Physical Universe'*
existence, or *beta-existence*, that the Physical
Body or *genetic vehicle* is essentially *anchored*
to for its considerations of locational space-time
as a dimension or POV.

facets : an aspect, an apparent phase; one of
many faces of something; a cut surface on a
gem or crystal; in *Systemology*—a single perception or aspect of a memory or "*Imprint*"; any
one of many ways in which a memory is recorded; perceptions associated with a painful emotional (sensation) experience and "*imprinted*"
onto a metaphoric lens through which to view

91

future similar experiences; other secondary terminals that are associated with a particular terminal, painful event or experience of loss, and which may exhibit the same encoded significance as the activating event.

feedback loop : a complete and continuous circuit flow of energy or information directed as an output from a source to a target which is altered and return back to the source as an input; in *General Systemology*—the continuous process where outputs of a system are routed back as inputs to complete a circuit or loop, which may be closed or connected to other systems/circuits; in *Systemology*—the continuous process where directed *Life* energy and *Awareness* is sent back to *Self* as experience, understanding and memory to complete an energetic circuit as a loop.

fragmentation : breaking into parts and scattering the pieces; the *fractioning* of wholeness or the *fracture* of a holistic interconnected *alpha* state, favoring observational *Awareness* of perceived connectivity between parts; *discontinuity*; separation of a totality into parts; in *Systemology*, a person outside a state of *Self-Honesty* is said to be *fragmented*.

genetic-vehicle : a physical *Life*-form; the physical (*beta*) body that is animated/controlled by the (*Alpha*) *Spirit* using a continuous *Lifeline* (ZU); a physical (*beta*) organic receptacle and catalyst for the (*Alpha*) *Self* to operate "causes" and experience "effects" within the *Physical Universe*.

gradient : a degree of partitioned ascent or descent along some scale, elevation or incline; "higher" and "lower" values in relation to one another.

holistic : the examination of interconnected systems as encompassing something greater than the *sum* of their "parts."

imagination : the ability to create *mental imagery* in one's Personal Universe at will and change or alter it as desired; the ability to create, change and dissolve mental images on command or as an act of will; to create a mental image or have associated imagery displayed (or "conjured") in the mind that may or may not be treated as real (or memory recall) and may or may not accurately duplicate objective reality; to employ *creative abilities* of the Spirit that are independent of reality agreements with beta-existence.

intention : directed application of Will; to intend (have "in Mind") or signify (give "significance" to) for or toward a particular purpose; in *Systemology* (from the *Standard Model*)—the spiritual activity at WILL (5.0) directed by an *Alpha Spirit* (7.0); the application of WILL as "Cause" from a higher order of Alpha Thought and consideration (6.0).

interior : inside of; on the inside; in *Systemology*, we mean specifically the POV of *Self* that is fixed to the *'internal' Human Condition,* including the *Reactive Control Center* (RCC) and Mind-System or *Master Control Center* (MCC); within *beta-existence*.

internal : a force coming from inside; information received from inside sources; in *Systemology*, the objective experience of *beta-existence* associated with the Physical Body or *genetic vehicle* and its POV regarding sensation and perception; from inside the body; in the body.

Human Condition : a standard default state of Human experience, generally accepted to be the extent of its potential identity (*beingness*).

imprint : to strongly impress, stamp, mark (or outline) onto a softer 'impressible' substance; to mark with pressure onto a surface; in *Systemology*, used to indicate permanent Reality impressions marked by frequencies, energies or interactions experienced during periods of emotional distress, pain, unconsciousness, loss, enforcement, or something antagonistic to physical (personal) survival, all of which are are stored with other reactive response-mechanisms at lower-levels of *Awareness* as opposed to the active memory database and proactive processing center of the Mind; an experiential "memory-set" that may later resurface—be triggered or stimulated artificially—as Reality, of which similar responses will be engaged automatically; holographic-like imagery "stamped" onto consciousness as composed of energetic *facets* tied to the "snap-shot" of an experience.

imprinting incident : the first or original event instance communicated and *emotionally encoded* onto an individual's "*Spiritual Timeline*" (recorded memory from all lifetimes), which formed a permanent impression that is later used to mechanistically treat future contact on that channel; the first or original occurrence of some particular *facet* or mental image related to a certain type of *encoded response*, such as pain and discomfort, losses and victimization, and even the acts that we have taken against others along the *Spiritual Timeline* of our existence that caused them to also be *Imprinted*.

knowledge : clear personal processing of informed understanding; information (data) that is actualized as effectively workable understanding; a demonstrable understanding on which we may 'set' our *Awareness*—or literally a "knowledge."

Master-Control-Center (MCC) : a perfect computing device to the extent of the information received from "lower levels" of sensory experience/perception; the proactive communication system of the "*Mind*"; a relay point of active *Awareness* along the Identity's *ZU-line*, which is responsible for maintaining basic *Self-Honest* clarity of *Knowingness* as a *seat of consciousness* between the *Alpha-Spirit* and the secondary "*Reactive Control Center*" of a *Life-form* in *beta existence*; the Mind-center for an *Alpha-Spirit* to actualize cause in the *beta existence*; the analytical *Self-Determined* Mind-center of an *Alpha-Spirit used* to project *Will* toward the genetic body; the point of contact between *Spiritual Systems* and the *beta existence*; presumably the "*Third Eye*" of a being connected directly to the *I-AM-Self*, which is responsible for *determining* Reality at any time; in *Systemology*, this is plotted at (4.0) on the continuity model of the *ZU-line*.

mental image : a subjectively experienced "picture" created and imagined into being by the Alpha-Spirit (or at lower levels, one of its automated mechanisms) that includes all perceptible *facets* of totally immersive scene, which may be forms originated by an individual, or a "facsimile-copy" ("snap-shot") of something seen or encountered; a duplication of wave-forms in one's Personal Universe as a "picture" that mirror an "external" Universe experience, such as an *Imprint*.

perception : internalized processing of data received by the *senses*; to become *Aware of* via the senses.

point-of-view (POV) : a point to view from; an opinion or attitude as expressed from a specific identity-phase; a specific standpoint or vantage-point; a definitive manner of consideration specific to an individual phase or identity; a place or position affording a specific view or vantage; circumstances and programming of an individual that is conducive to a particular response, consideration or belief-set (paradigm); a position (consideration) or place (location) that provides a specific view or perspective (subjective) on experience (of the objective). May also be referred to in our texts as a "*viewpoint.*"

processing, systematic : the inner-workings or "through-put" result of systems; in *Systemology*, a methodology of applied spiritual technology used toward personal Self-Actualization; methods of selective directed attention, communicated language and associative imagery that targets an increase in personal control of the human condition.

reactive control center (RCC) : the secondary (reactive) communication system of the "*Mind*"; a relay point of *Awareness* along the Identity's *ZU-line*, which is responsible for engaging basic motors, biochemical processes and any *programmed automated responses* of a living *beta* organism; the reactive Mind-Center of a living organism relaying communications of *Awareness* between causal experience of *Physical Systems* and the "*Master Control Center*"; it presumably stores all emotional encoded imprints as fragmentation of *ZU* (within the range of the "*psychological/ emotive systems*" of a being), which it may *react* to as Reality at any time; in *Systemology*, this is plotted at (2.0) on the continuity model of the *ZU-line*.

reality : see "*agreement.*"

Seeker : an individual on the *Pathway to Self-Honesty*; a practitioner of *Mardukite Systemology* or *Systemology Processing* that is working toward *Spiritual Ascension*.

Self-actualization : bringing the full potential of the Human spirit into Reality; expressing full capabilities and creativeness of the *Alpha-Spirit*.

Self-determinism : the freedom to act, clear of external control or influence; the personal control of Will to direct intention.

Self-honesty : the basic or original *alpha* state of *being* and *knowing*; clear and present total *Awareness* of-and-as *Self*, in its most basic and true proactive expression of itself as *Spirit* or *I-AM*—free of artificial attachments, perceptive filters and other emotionally-reactive or mentally-conditioned programming imposed on the human condition by the systematized physical world; the ability to experience existence without judgment.

sensation : an external stimulus received by internal sense organs (receptors/sensors); sense impressions.

slate : a hard thin flat surface material used for writing on; a chalk-board, which is a large version of the original wood-framed writing slate, named for the rock-type it was made from.

Spheres of Existence (dynamic systems) : a model of *eight* concentric circles, rings or spheres (each larger than the former) that is overlaid onto the Standard Model of Beta-Existence to demonstrate dynamic systems of existence extending out from a POV of Self (often as a "body") at the *First Sphere*; these are given as a basic eightfold system: *Self, Home/Family, Groups, Humanity, Life on Earth, Physical Universe, Spiritual Universe* and *Infinity-Divinity.*

spiritual timeline : a continuous stream of moment-to-moment *Mental Images* (or a record of experiences) that defines the "past" of a spiritual being (or *Alpha-Spirit*) and which includes impressions (*imprints, &tc.*) form all life-incarnations and significant spiritual events the being has encountered.

Standard Model, The (systemology) : our existential and cosmological *standard model* or cabbalistic model; a "*monistic continuity model*" demonstrating *total system* interconnectivity "above" and "below" observation of any apparent *parameters*; the original presentation of the *ZU-line*, represented as a singular vertical (*y*-axis) waveform in space across dimensional levels or Universes (*Spheres of Existence*) without charting any specific movement across a dimensional time-graph *x*-axis; The Standard Model of Systemology represents the basic workable synthesis of common denominators in models explored throughout Grade-I and Grade-II material.

system : from the Greek, "to set together"; to set or arrange things or data together so as to form an orderly understanding of a "whole."

terminal (node) : a point, end or mass on a line; a point or connection for closing an electric circuit, such as a post on a battery terminating at each end of its own systematic function; any end point or 'termination' on a line; a point of connectivity with other points; in systems, any point which may be treated as a contact point of interaction; anything that may be distinguished as an 'is' and is therefore a 'termination point' of a system or along a flow-line which may interact with other related systems it shares a line with; a point of interaction with other points.

thought-form : apparent *manifestation* or existential *realization* of *Thought-waves* as "solids" even when only apparent in Reality-agreements of the Observer; the treatment of *Thought-waves* as permanent *imprints* obscuring *Self-Honest* clarity of *Awareness* when reinforced by emotional experience as actualized "thought-formed solids" ("*beliefs*") in the Mind; energetic patterns that "surround" the individual.

ZU : the ancient Sumerian cuneiform sign for the archaic verb—"*to know*," "*knowingness*" or "*awareness*"; in *Mardukite Zuism and Systemology*, the active energy/matter of the "Spiritual Universe" (AN) experienced as a *Lifeforce* or *consciousness* that imbues living forms extant in the "Physical Universe" (KI); "*Spiritual Life Energy*"; energy demonstrated by the WILL of an actualized *Alpha-Spirit* in the "Spiritual Universe" (AN), which impinges its *Awareness* into the Physical Universe (KI), animating/controlling *Life* for its experience of *beta-existence* along an individual Alpha-Spirit's personal *Identity-continuum*, called a *ZU-line*.

Zu-Line : a theoretical construct in *Mardukite Zuism and Systemology* demonstrating *Spiritual Life Energy* (*ZU*) as a personal individual "continuum" of Awareness interacting with all Spheres of Existence on the Standard Model of Systemology; a spectrum of potential variations and interactions of a monistic continuum or singular *Spiritual Life Energy (ZU)* demonstrated on the Standard Model; an energetic channel of potential POV and "locations" of Beingness, demonstrated in early Systemology materials as an individual Alpha-Spirit's personal *Identity-continuum*, potentially connecting *Awareness (ZU)* of *Self* with "*Infinity*" simultaneous with all points considered in existence; a symbolic demonstration of the "*Life-line*" on which *Awareness (ZU)* extends from the direction of the "Spiritual Universe" (AN) in its true original *alpha state* through an entire possible range of activity resulting in its *beta state* and control of a *genetic-entity* occupying the *Physical Universe (KI)*.

complete your study of the
Fundamentals of Systemology
with all six
Basic Course Lesson Booklets

Lesson #1
BEING MORE THAN HUMAN
Rediscovering the Spiritual Self

Lesson #2
REALITIES IN AGREEMENT
Spiritual Life and The Universe

Lesson #3
WINDOWS TO EXPERIENCE
The Filters of Human Perception

Lesson #4
ANCIENT SYSTEMOLOGY
Wisdom From the Arcane Tablets

Lesson #5
A HISTORY OF SYSTEMOLOGY
Evolution of a Spiritual Science

Lesson #6
SYSTEMOLOGY PROCESSING
Practices of Spiritual Awakening

THE SYSTEMOL

Seekers and students of the *Basic Course* and *Professional Course* will also be interested in the *Advanced Series* of the *Systemology Core*. These volumes are a complete chronological record of the Mardukite New Thought developments from the Systemology Society, published in 2019 through 2023.

The *Systemology Core* begins with the first professional publication released when the *Mardukite Systemology Society* emerged from the underground in 2019, with: *"The Tablets of Destiny Revelation."*

OGY PATHWAY

The Tablets of Destiny Revelation:
*How Long-Lost Anunnaki Wisdom
Can Change the Fate of Humanity*

Crystal Clear: *Handbook for Seekers*

Metahuman Destinations (*2 volumes*)

Imaginomicon:
Approaching Gateways to Higher Universes

Way of the Wizard: *Utilitarian Systemology*

Systemology-180: *Fast-Track to Ascension*

Systemology Backtrack:
Reclaiming Spiritual Power & Past-Life Memory

PUBLISHED BY THE **JOSHUA FREE** IMPRINT REPRESENTING

The Mardukite Academy of Systemology

THE JOSHUA FREE IMPRINT
JFI PUBLICATIONS

MARDUKITE
ZUISM

mardukite.com

www.ingramcontent.com/pod-product-compliance
Lightning Source LLC
Chambersburg PA
CBHW071207120626
46546CB00006B/2456

One 'n Done #10

BROOKLYN
FAMILY
ALBUM

A memoir by
Margaret Montet

Published by

Read Often. Read Well.

Published by Read Furiously - Trenton, NJ. First
Edition.

ISBN: 978-1-960869-11-1
Library of Congress Control Number: 2024945018

Memoir
Personal History
New York City

For more information on *Brooklyn Family Album* or Read
Furiously, please visit readfuriously.com. For inquiries,
please contact info@readfuriously.com.